The Miraculous Medal

By Mary Goggins

Copyright © 2019 by Mary Goggins.

All rights reserved. No parts of this publication 'The Miraculous Medal' may be reproduced, stored in a retrieval system or transmitted in any form or by any means, without the prior written permission of the author, nor be otherwise circulated in any form of binding or cover other than that in which it is published and without a similar condition being imposed by the purchaser. This book is intended for your personal use only. All views are the authors and the author and publisher assume no responsibility for any errors or omissions. The content of this publication is for personal enjoyment only and not in an advisory capacity. Publishing services by Orla Kelly Publishing Services.

This book is dedicated to my loving family and to my dear friend, Jim

Acknowledgements

I would like to thank my publisher Orla Kelly for all of her wonderful help in assisting me to get this book published. I would like to thank my family for their understanding, support and encouragement. I would also like to thank my dear friend Jim for his kindness and love.

Contents

Dedication	iii
Acknowledgements	v
My Journey Towards Happiness	1
Mary Virgin Mother of Our Lord Jesus	5
The History of the Miraculous Medal	10
True stories of people who wore the Miraculous Medal	14
Final Thoughts	22
About the Author	25
Other Books by the Author	26

My Journey Towards Happiness

The path that I took in life since leaving secondary school had been one of strife and discord. From being a stressed-out student to a stressed-out executive, I was wound up, worn out and weary.

My life gradually began to change when some years ago, I was invited to join the Legion of Mary in my local town in Ireland. The Legion of Mary is a devoted group of followers of Mary, the Mother of God, who meet weekly to say the Rosary, recite prayers and talk about their dedication to Our Lady through their work and their lives. They give unselfishly of their time and efforts to show their affection for Mary, Our Mother, and to further Her message of love in the world.

I began to wear the miraculous medal that I received from the Legion of Mary, and since then my life has gently and most assuredly become happier and brighter.

I have become clearer and more positive in my deliberations. I am cheerful and filled with hope and tend to show more thoughtfulness and steadfastness than before.

I do not get agitated or anxious as much as I did, and I cast all my worries and concerns on Our Lord Jesus and His Mother Mary.

I do not let the weight of the burdens of life overshadow me. Instead, I gently hold the Miraculous Medal and take comfort in the security of knowing that Our Lady will take care of it.

I feel more carefree, and I know that whatever trouble or difficulty comes my way, I can ask Mother Mary for help with it, and she will help me.

I was healed by Our Lady, and I will always be thankful to Her for Her guidance, friendship and consolation.

Our Lady promised great graces for all who wear the Miraculous Medal. Mother Mary also promised that many graces would also be bestowed on all who evangelise for the Lord and on all who share the Miraculous Medal with others.

Mary Queen of Heaven

Oh Mary, Queen of Heaven, My Holy and Immaculate Mother,
You are an exquisite Mediatrix,
By your shining example,
And by your clear and star-filled light,
Through the beauty of your heart,
And through your eternal and undying love,
Filled gratefully with your peaceful graces,
Graciously grant that I may be an instrument of your goodness in the world.

The Miraculous Medal

Oh Mary, Holy Mother of the Saviour of the world,
You gave precious life to the greatest joy this world has ever known,
Your maternal care and true devotion,
In times of happiness and sadness,
Has forever won our hearts
Because even when life was difficult, you always said yes to God.
Oh Mary, my caring and sweet Mother,
Your deep concern for me,
And your loving protection,
Has helped me to find my way in a sometimes complex and confusing world,
Let me more than mundanely live,
Let me sparkle in your love,
Let me be overjoyed by your kindness,
Let me smile because of your infinite tenderness,
And let me stand tall and strong in the face of adversity;
And when I wear this most precious Miraculous Medal,
Let me think of you and your life with Jesus and Saint Joseph
In Nazareth so long ago,
And may I treasure this forever.
Amen.

Mary Goggins

Mary Virgin Mother of Our Lord Jesus

Mary, the Mother of God, is the Mother of Jesus, Mother of the Church and Mother of us all. She is the caring Mother of Our Saviour Jesus born in a stable in Bethlehem two thousand years ago. She was there with Jesus throughout the great joys of his youth and by his side in times of pain. Her maternal qualities of tenderness and compassion endear her to us, and we both admire and respect her because of her endurance and long-suffering for the special and noble life of her Son Jesus.

Jesus was a man of very many spiritual gifts, and He performed many remarkable miracles. He was magnificent and his rare and unique spiritual powers have left its mark on this world such that the world has never known before. He is a gift to Humanity. Jesus was a sympathetic teacher and friend. His human nature and caring life and deep mercy for the weak, the lonely, the suffering and the outcast make him a man filled with deep love and affection for humankind. He was love. He was life.

Just like Jesus, Mary is meek and mild, humble and true. Her heart and mind are pure. Her deeply loving and eternal qualities and grace unveil Her view of the world and Her message for the sometimes dark and painful reality in which we live.

What is the message that Mary our mother In Heaven has for the human race?

Our Lady wants us to turn to God with all of our hardships and difficulties in life and to depend on Him. She wants us to pray about everything. She wants us to turn to Jesus her Son with humbleness of heart and to ask for His help in all things. She wants us to be happy, to live more simply, and to live with and for one another and not against one another. She wants us to cooperate rather than compete and to take care of each other. She wants us to be healed and to forgive one another. She wants us to be merciful to one another and to remember each other in times of need and to call on one another. She wants us to care for our elders and our children too and to be concerned about everyone.

Life is not about trying to get ahead of everyone else or elevating the ego or going after excessive money or power but instead about living with virtues, grace and peace. She wants us to keep the Commandments and to take care of the world. She wants us to look after each other when tragedy strikes and to keep Jesus and all of the Saints and Angels in Heaven forever in our hearts and to call on them when we need them.

She wants us to work to save the world, not to destroy it and to become apostles of her love.

This can be done through prayer and Our Lady's intercession. To help us, many times on this earth, Our Lady has appeared as an Apparition to holy people in special places.

Some examples of these places include Knock in County Mayo in Ireland; Medjugorje in Bosnia Herzegovina; Fatima in Portugal; Lourdes in France; and Guadaloupe in Mexico.

When Our Lady makes an Apparition, she comes with a special message. Sometimes it's to warn us of danger in our world to protect us and sometimes it's a message of hope asking us to pray and reminding us of who we are and who we always were as children of God.

The message of Mary and Jesus Her Son is one of eternal love, great sorrow, care for every person, and of deep compassion. Mary wants to guide us home to Her Son Jesus where we can love as Jesus loves and live joyously and eternally as He lives.

Prayer To Our Lady

Mary My Mother of Heaven and of Earth,
Each day I pray
That you will be with me always,
And that you will be there to guide me on my life's journey.
I pray that I will forever be influenced
By your holiness and grace
And by your sanctity and devotion and love for Jesus.
May your life of perfection and virtue
Inspire me
To live more fully
And to love completely
With all my heart.
Amen.

The Miraculous Medal

The History of the Miraculous Medal

As mentioned earlier, over the course of history, Our Lady Mary Mother of God has made apparitions to many blessed people in sacred places. One such holy person was Catherine Laboure who was a novice with the Daughters of Charity of the Saint Vincent de Paul. On July 18th 1830, at about midnight, Catherine Laboure had a vision of the Mother of God while in the chapel of the Rue de Bac in Paris, France.

On November 27th 1830, Our Lady appeared again and showed Catherine the medal of The Immaculate Conception later to be known as the Miraculous Medal. Our Lady asked Catherine to have this medal made for Her. Our Lady showed Catherine the design of the medal. The medal was to be for all who wore it a sign of Our Lady's protection and love in the world which She offers to each one of us.

By wearing the medal, it demonstrated a gesture of acceptance of Our Lady. The medal became known as the miraculous medal because of the wonderful acts of kindness and love that came from Our Lady upon those who wore it.

The design of the medal that Our Lady gave to Catherine Laboure, showed on the front a woman, The Mother of God, with the words 'Oh Mary conceived without sin pray for us who have recourse to thee.'

The Miraculous Medal

On it, Mary stands on a globe which is 'the world.' Around her feet, a twisted serpent representing 'the devil' struggling for supremacy. This represents the conflict between good and evil. Mary's world is one of light, peace, and grace and Satan's world is one of darkness, shame and disgrace. But the victory belongs to Mary won by Christ, who is the light of the world. This is shown by the light and grace of Christ flowing from her hands.

On the back of the medal, there is a letter M with a cross above it. M is for Mary and Mother as Mary is the Mother of God. The 12 stars around the sides of the medal symbolise the 12 apostles. The two hearts are those of Jesus and Mary. Mary's heart is pierced by a sword which symbolises her suffering while the heart of Jesus is pierced by a soldier's lance.

The medal is not a good luck charm. It is a reminder that Our Lady will help us, lighten our darkness and give us hope.

Our Lady asked Catherine for an altar to be built at the location of the apparitions, and a statue made showing Our Lady holding a globe representing the world and offering it to God.

At the time of the apparitions in 1830, only Catherine's spiritual director knew of Catherine's visions of Our Lady. For 47 years, Catherine lived an ordinary life as a Daughter of Charity until she finally told one of her superiors of the apparitions. Since that time, the Daughters of Charity and Vincentian Fathers have promoted the medal and its message of love to the world.

Catherine Laboure died on December 31st, 1876. She was canonised on July 27th 1947 by Pope Pius XII and her feast day is November 28th.

Prayer for all who wear the Miraculous Medal

I, Mary Mother of Jesus
Offer you this Medal
As a sign of my maternal and everlasting love for the world.
May all who wear this miraculous medal
Experience the light of Christ
And His love in their hearts.
May peace and joy reign in your lives,
May you be filled with hope,
And I pray that you will always be protected.
Amen.

True stories of people who wore the Miraculous Medal

There are many wonderful stories of miracles and unexplained and happy events recorded by people who wear the miraculous medal. We cherish these stories.

There are joyous accounts from those who wore the medal who have reported that their burdens and sorrows were removed, their anxiety and depression was completely gone, their lives transformed and their difficulties turned around. There have been healings of the sick, assistance with practical and temporal needs and hope in times of despair.

One of the most remarkable stories of the intercession of Our Lady through wearing the miraculous medal is the story of Claude Newman.

Claude Newman was an African American man who was born on December 1st 1923. At a young age, Claude was brought with his older brother to live with their grandmother Ellen Newman. Claude's grandmother married a man named Sid Cook and the relationship between Claude and Sid broke down when Sid became sexually abusive to Claude's grandmother. Sid and Ellen later separated. However, Claude was still very angry with Sid, and he wanted revenge. On December 19th 1942, Claude waited for Sid at his house, and shot him as he entered the house. In addition to murdering Sid, Claude also stole money from his pocket. Claude was later arrested, prosecuted, sent to prison and put on death row.

While Claude was in jail, he shared a prison cell with other prisoners. One night while some of the prisoners were sitting and talking, Claude noticed a medal on a string around one prisoner's neck. Claude was curious as to what the medal meant, and the other prisoner suddenly cast off the medal and threw it on the floor at Claude's feet telling Claude to take it.

Claude picked up the medal and placed it around his neck unaware of the significance of the medal. Somehow Claude felt drawn to the medal and wanted to wear it.

Claude went to sleep that night, and during the night, he had a vision from the Virgin Mary Mother of God. He felt a light touch on his wrist, and he awoke to see what he described as 'the most beautiful woman that God ever created.'

The Virgin Mary told Claude 'If you would like me to be your Mother and you would like to be my child, send for a priest of the Catholic Church.' Then the vision disappeared.

Claude asked to see a Catholic priest and the priest who came was Father Robert O'Leary SVD. Claude told the priest what happened and also told the other prisoners in his cell. They asked for religious instruction in the Catholic faith.

Claude knew very little about religious teaching, so the priest began instructing him about Jesus and the Catholic faith. Claude received the sacrament of Confession and the Sacrament of Holy Communion. After Claude and the other prisoners finished the religious instruction they were received into the Catholic Church. Claude was baptised on January 16th 1944.

The time was approaching for Claude to be executed for his crime. He was to be executed at 5 minutes after midnight on January 20th 1944. The sheriff asked Claude if he had any last requests. Claude reportedly said 'You don't understand. I am not sad. I'm not going to die. It's only this body. I am going to be with the Mother of God. So then, I would like to have a party.' Claude asked for permission for the priest to throw a party with cakes and ice cream for him and the other prisoners. The warden consented, and they were permitted a party. After the party, Claude asked for a holy hour to pray for him and all their souls. The other prisoners returned to their cells and Claude was given the Holy Eucharist before his execution. Just before Claude was due to be executed, the sheriff came running towards Claude's cell and said that there would be a reprieve for two weeks. Claude was unaware that the sheriff and district attorney were applying for a stay of execution and he started to cry. He said 'But you don't understand. If you ever saw her face and looked into her eyes you wouldn't want to live another day.'

Claude was broken-hearted that he could not die and be with the Blessed Mary. He loved her that much. Claude was in tears. Father O'Leary consoled him and asked him to offer this denial as a sacrifice for the conversion of another prisoner named James Hughes, who was a white prisoner sentenced to execution for murder. James Hughes rejected God completely and all things Christian. Claude reflected on this, and he agreed and offered sacrifice and prayers for James Hughes.

Two weeks later, on February 4th 1944, Claude was executed by electric chair. Father O'Leary said of Claude's holy death 'I have never seen anyone go to his death as joyfully and happily.' Even the official witnesses and the newspaper reporters were amazed and said they 'couldn't understand how anyone could go to the electric chair and yet be beaming with happiness.'

Three months later, on May 19th 1944, the white man James Hughes was to be executed. He had hated God and all things spiritual. Just before his execution, the county doctor pleaded with him to at least say the Our Father prayer. The condemned man spat in his face. When strapped to the electric chair, the sheriff said to him 'if you have anything to say, say it now.'

The prisoner looked around the room and suddenly started to scream. Turning to the sheriff, he said 'get me to a priest.' Father O'Leary was present, and he heard confession. He confessed that he had been a Catholic but had turned away from his religion due to his immoral ways. He confessed his sins with deep sorrow and repentance.

When the confession was over the sheriff asked him what had changed his mind. Why had he suddenly turned to God in his final moments when he was blaspheming that he hated God all his life.

The prisoner replied 'Do you remember that man named Claude Newman? I have just seen a vision of him standing in the corner of the room and behind him was the Blessed Virgin Mary. Claude said in the vision that he had offered his death in union with Christ on the cross for my salvation and that the Blessed Virgin Mary had obtained for me this gift of seeing my place in Hell if I do not repent. I saw my place in Hell, and that's why I screamed.'

The heavenly vision of Our Lady and Claude Newman and the vision of Hell had converted James Hughes' soul in the last moments of his life before his execution.

Claude Newman had offered his suffering in union with the suffering of Christ, and by making prayers and sacrifice for the conversion of James Hughes, he had helped to pay the price of his last-minute conversion and confession. James Hughes soul was saved from final damnation.

Claude Newman's discovery of the miraculous medal had opened up a different world to him. A new world of hope, happiness and joy. God had forgiven him all that he had done, and through the beautiful intercession of Our Lady, he could look forward to eternal life. He could hardly wait to be with the Blessed Mother Mary and the profound promise of his home in heaven.

The Miraculous Medal

Another sacred story of the intercession of Our Lady through the wearing of the miraculous medal is the story of Saint Maximilian Kolbe. Maximilian Maria Kolbe was born as Raymond Kolbe in Poland on January 8th 1894.

When he was just a boy, Our Lady appeared to him in a dream. In the dream, Our Lady was holding a white crown and a red crown. She asked young Kolbe if he was willing to accept either crown. The white one meant that he could persevere in purity and the red one meant that he could become a martyr. Kolbe, with deep love, told Our Lady that he would accept them both.

This was to be a great prophecy for his life because when he grew up, he became a Franciscan novice and was ordained as a Franciscan Friar in 1918. He had great faith and devotion to Our Lady.

With deep love and affection he wore the miraculous medal, and promoted the veneration of the Immaculate Virgin Mary. He was the founder of Militia Immaculatae which means the 'Army of the Immaculate One' which is a worldwide Catholic evangelisation movement.

During World War II, he volunteered to die at the young age of 47 in place of a stranger sentenced to death in the German concentration camp of Auschwitz.

He was declared a Martyr of Charity and was canonised on October 10th 1982 by Pope John Paul II. He is known as the Patron Saint of the twentieth century. Saint Maximilian Kolbe had given his life to God and in service and love to

The Miraculous Medal

Mary, Our Mother with 'no greater love than to lay down his life for his friends.'

Final Thoughts

The miraculous medal is a wonderful sacramental (This is an object or action used in our faith to show religious devotion). Many people who wear the medal receive great blessings, including cures for illnesses and miraculous conversions. Wearing the miraculous medal shows true devotion to Our Lady and Jesus, Our Lord.

Below are two prayers which can be recited when wearing the Miraculous Medal.

The Miraculous Medal Prayer

Oh Mary conceived without sin pray for us who have recourse to you and for all who do not have recourse to you, especially the enemies of the church and those recommended to you.

Amen.

(The first part of this prayer was given by Our Lady to Saint Catherine Laboure and the second part of this prayer was added by Maximillian Kolbe).

Second Miraculous Medal Prayer

Oh Virgin Mother of God Mary Immaculate we dedicate and consecrate ourselves to you under the title of Our Lady of the Miraculous Medal. May this medal be for each of us a sure sign of your affection for us and a constant reminder of our duties toward you. Ever while wearing it may we be blessed by your loving protection and preserved in the grace of your Son. Oh most powerful Virgin Mother of our Saviour keep us close to you every moment of our lives. Obtain for us your children the grace of a happy death so that in union with you, we may enjoy the bliss of heaven forever. Amen.

By wearing the miraculous medal, it represents to the world our love and fidelity toward Mary Our Mother and Her Son Jesus. It helps to defend us from the snares of Satan, and it protects us from harm. Remember to wear it rather than leaving it down on a table or dresser. Mary prefers us to wear it. Mary Our Mother knows her children. Don't be ashamed to wear it. Don't be afraid to wear it. And may God reward you and keep you. And may the love of Jesus and Mary always be forever in your hearts.

If any person would like to receive a blessed miraculous medal they can email the author at miraculousmedal19@gmail.com and I would be very happy to send them one. Any person from any background, tradition, faith or walk of life can wear the miraculous medal.

I pray that it will bring you great blessings. May it bring peace and healing to you. Let it bring you miracles and laughter. May it bring you love and acceptance. And may whatever you carry in life be lifted from you by Mother Mary so that Her love transcends all pain, all despair, all hardships, all difficulties and you are set free.

The End

About the Author

The author of this book, Mary Goggins, is a devout Catholic and a Eucharistic Minister, and her purpose is to find a way to bring sacred healing to our fragile humanity.

Other Books by the Author

Christian Healing

How to Be Successful in Life

The Blessed Sacrament

Sparkle amd Shine

Available from Amazon.

Made in United States
Cleveland, OH
14 July 2025

18342303R10024